MW00890001

IN LOVING MEMORY OF

APOSTLE DON STEWART

This man of God generously dedicated time from his busy schedule to mentor me in international ministry. In April 2018, he graciously invited me to be a guest speaker at his 53rd anniversary celebration in Alaminos, Philippines. Apostle Don consistently provided invaluable guidance, even reaching out to me while I was on the road in my 18-wheeler, offering insightful pointers and advice to enhance my ministry. His teachings, particularly about the workings of the Holy Spirit, have profoundly impacted me. In 2017, Apostle Don wrote the foreword for my book, "Awakening the Inner Man," and warmly welcomed me into his international ministry. The influence of this remarkable man of God on the world is immeasurable, and I wholeheartedly believe that he has ascended to Heaven's pearly gates, eagerly anticipating my arrival when I cross over.

A DAY AFTER SALVATION

All Scripture, unless otherwise indicated, is taken from the King James translation of the bible.

ISBN: 9798854499279

Printed in the United States of America
Title: **A Day After Salvation**
Author: **Jerry W. Hulse, Ph.D.**
Editor & Cover: **Augustina M. Hulse**
Total Pages: 96
Second Printing Revised Edition
Non-Fiction – Self-help / Inspiration / Religion
Suitable to readers of all ages

A DAY AFTER SALVATION

Revised Edition

Table of Contents

OPENING PRAYER

Father, I pray in Jesus' name, recognizing his great sacrifice at Calvary, that your honor and glory be manifested in this work of faith, and may your countenance smile through it to strengthen the redeemed, that souls may be added to your kingdom. Dear Lord, I ask that your hand be upon this work of faith, and may your HOLY SPIRIT'S presence anoint this work to touch the hearts of everyone who will take time out of their busy schedule to absorb its truths. Father, I ask you, yes, Lord, to charge your assigned ministering Angels to accompany this work of faith as posted guards, removing any hindrances that would come against this work, that you use this work to show the people that you are the unchanging God, for Lord, your word declares that what you were yesterday, you are today, and will be tomorrow. (Hebrews 13:8)

Dear Lord, please help us realize our dependence is upon you. Therefore, Lord, help us know that we are a part of your glorious body on earth; help us understand that there is strength in numbers; and help us see that we need each other to be fruitful and to live a prosperous life as your people. Father God, help us not be careless and prideful in our Christian Walk, but help us realize, Lord, that we are a part of something bigger than ourselves; we are a part of your glorious body on earth recognized as sons and daughters in your kingdom.

Heavenly Father, I am deeply grateful for the opportunity to say a word of prayer for all who will take time out of their busy schedule to read this prayer with an open heart. I ask that you bless each person spiritually, financially, physically, relationally, and emotionally so that their life may be blessed to enrich the lives of others. From this day forward, I ask that your will, your word, your purpose, your will, and your Spirit have free course in their lives and those of everyone they may meet; that you will touch, heal, and deliver all who read this prayer and call upon your blessed name.

Father, I pray that you will meet the needs of all who read this book right where they are, that all curses and words spoken against them will be broken, and that they may prosper in all they do for your kingdom. Dear Lord, I ask that you stand up inside them and awaken their gifts and talents from birth so they may become unified in the faith with other believers, realizing the need to work together in harmony like a fine-tuned orchestra in the masters' hands. Dear Heavenly Father, thank you for your tremendous love and blessing over our lives. We rest knowing that you promised never to leave nor forsake us as your children. Lord, you promised to go with us all the way, even to the end of the world, which is a great comfort in knowing that whatever we may be called to go through in life, we do not have to go through these trials alone. Dear Lord, we ask that you enlarge our borders and place your hand upon us to guide us in your chosen path.

Father, we need your divine guidance to lead us by your Spirit to divine appointments. Lord, we ask that you please deliver us from evil so we will not be tempted or cause pain. Lord, I pray that your blessed holy name might be glorified throughout the earth as you leave your signature through us to future generations. Lord, I ask that you assign an Angel to accompany this work into the homes of every person who will take the time to read it.

Father God, please help us stand firm together, activating our faith, for it is in these trying times, through your grace, that we can find rest in knowing that we can depend on you, our God, "Our Father," to come on the scene to direct our path and to guide our footsteps, helping us to understand that our dependence for survival is upon you. Dear Lord, help us realize that we represent your glorious body on earth; therefore, help us know that there is strength in numbers, and we need each other to be fruitful so that we can live prosperous lives as your people. Lord, I pray that You stir us up for revival in every country throughout the world, demonstrating to the people in these countries that You are the Unchanging God, for Your word declares that what you were yesterday, you are today and will be tomorrow! (Hebrews 13:8) Heavenly Father, I pray that if any of the people reading this prayer should need deliverance from some oppressing spirit, including some illnesses that may be attacking their body, Lord, I pray that your Holy Spirit would raise a standard against these attacks and set them free.

Dear Lord, thank you for hearing my humble, sincere prayer. I pray that the power of your word is activated to all who need encouragement and that it is activated through the authority made available to us in the blessed name of Jesus. Lord, I wish to apply the following scriptures to my prayer, believing that you have heard and answered me according to your divine will and purpose, for it is in the mighty name of Jesus that I pray and ask these favors. A-Men

(John 16:23) "And in that day ye shall ask me nothing. Verily, I say unto you, Whatsoever ye shall ask the father in my name, he will give it to you."

(Psalms 34:15) "The eyes of the LORD are upon the righteous, and his ears are open unto their cry."

FOREWORD

Ludy Benedicto Capapas, BTh

Store Branch Manager

PHILIPPINE CHRISTIAN BOOKSTORE(PCBS)
(SM Fairview, Quezon City Metro Manila, Philippines)

I am delighted to endorse the enlightening book, "A Day After Salvation," by Evangelist and Christian author Dr. Jerry W. Hulse. The author's profound insights skillfully guide the reader to a deeper understanding of God as a loving and forgiving Father, unlike the unforgiving world around us. His emphasis on building a relationship with God through various illustrations is enlightening. After reading the first few chapters of this manuscript, I can confidently say that it has empowered and elevated me to another level. The meaning of life and its sacred origin have puzzled scholars since the "Genesis" of time and are beautifully addressed in this manuscript. It leads you to a spiritually enriched conclusion that life is a sacred gift.

I have only known Dr. Jerry and his beautiful wife, Augustina, for over two years, but during those two years, we have become good friends. Each time they visit our bookstore, a peaceful atmosphere seems to linger even after they leave. When Dr. Jerry and Augustina are in our store, some of our customers love to fellowship with them, and after they leave, we receive positive feedback informing us of how they were blessed to be in their presence. After reading this book and looking at the condition of the church today, I am prompted to ask an essential question that I feel needs to be addressed, and that is, "Are you going to be a spectator in the bleachers, or are you going to become a soldier on the battlefield for Christ?"

Many people today are troubled and seeking answers in the face of the challenges on Earth. A few have come to our bookstore looking for a reason to live and often ask, "Does God Love Me?" The author's words provide reassurance and comfort, affirming that our God is Omnipotent, "All-powerful," Omniscient, "All-knowing," and "All-loving." He has plans for our life before we are born. Christ is actively building his church on Earth, which is his body, offering hope and a reason to live.

Because God's love for us as his children is a pure love that has been tested, we can embrace the cross with confidence and face the trials of life, allowing them to strengthen and bind us together as one unified body because God's love is an unconditional love that the plans and schemes of the enemy cannot shake.

This book does an excellent job of encouraging Christians to rise and take a stand for Jesus. It beautifully advises us to unlock the door to our hearts, allowing Jesus to enter our lives and guide us into the right path. In this book, the author exposes the way of our world today in which Christians seem to have forgotten their first love, including the true purpose and calling of the church on Earth.

The most important part of this book is the author's emphasis that newborn Christians who have never been to church cannot be expected to know what mature Christians know about God.

Reading this book with a prayerful heart and an open mind can catalyze spiritual growth. It sheds light on the current state of the church. The author's message is clear: God's love for humanity, his most magnificent creation, is so profound that he sacrificed his only Son for our redemption and salvation. The book's ability to inspire spiritual growth motivates and encourages readers to persevere, especially in these challenging times. The author skillfully utilized Bible verses to connect each message, assuring readers that the teachings were not motivated by the author's pursuit of personal fame. The way the author delivered the messages in this inspiring book can be pure revival to a hungry soul because they are amazingly composed with energy and excitement that will elevate you to feel your soul start to move with every word you may read slowly.

As members of the body of Christ, we must recognize the unseen battle between good and evil that surrounds us. This book is a powerful tool to unite us in our shared faith and purpose. It is a must-read for anyone who will allow its teachings to enrich their lives and desire more of God in their lives and ministries.

I read the first printed edition, which was filled with inspirational teachings. I appreciated how the author addressed the need for follow-up ministry in individuals who have just accepted Christ. The revised version strongly emphasizes the importance of staying committed to prayer and remaining vigilant against attacks from the enemy, particularly for those dedicated to living a Christian life.

I wholeheartedly invite you to join us in our journey as we explore these inspired writings and embrace our purpose in "A Day After Salvation." I highly recommend this book as an essential addition to any library. If you are in the Philippines, be sure to visit a PCBS bookstore and greet our staff. Also, don't hesitate to ask for prayer if you need it, as we collaborate closely with local pastors who visit our stores. Ludy Benedicto Capapas, BTh

PREFACE

This book is written to connect with individuals who do not regularly attend church, particularly those living on the streets in a world that has seemingly lost sight of the value of life. We decided not to capitalize satan's name throughout this book because we do not believe he deserves recognition. Some schools are known to teach evolution instead of creation, which results in a generation that does not place value on life.

Salvation is a profound and pivotal point in an individual's spiritual journey, signifying the acceptance of God's forgiveness and grace through the sacrifice of Jesus Christ. It is a transformative and deeply personal experience that marks the beginning of a lifelong commitment to following Christ's teachings, emulating his example, and aligning one's life with the principles and will of God. Salvation represents a turning point, leading to a life of faith, service, and obedience by the Christian faith.

This book explores the intricate workings of salvation, probing into how it awakens a person's spirit and liberates them from the power of sin. It also examines some individuals' ongoing struggles with sinful habits. It is a powerful resource for any church ministry that earnestly seeks to reach out to a world in pain and confusion, offering them answers and a purposeful life through the teachings of Christianity.

As I prayerfully begin this book, I have thoughts of a young lady who had several children, but one evening, the young lady pulled into a church parking lot and ended her life because, to her, she ran out of reasons to live. What happens to those who've just given their lives over to the Lord, and has the thought ever entered your mind, "Did they believe what they just prayed," or "Will they be able to stand the onslaught that is surely coming?"

It's essential to recognize that new converts who have recently dedicated their lives to Christ are not expected to have the same understanding as those who have been on their faith journey for a long time. They need our patience and guidance as they start their spiritual journey. Let's walk alongside them, offering unwavering support and deep understanding as they navigate the challenges and joys of their newfound faith. Let's be their pillars of strength, their beacons of hope, and their sources of comfort.

This book's valuable teaching will help prepare new converts for life's many trials. Remember, God is with us every step of the way to strengthen and encourage those struggling in their faith. His grace is available to all who call upon his blessed, holy name. So, take comfort in His guidance and support, knowing you are never alone in your spiritual journey. Did you know there are people today who claim that when they gave their life to Christ, all sinful cravings were instantly taken away from them? In their pride, these people tend to look down on others, still struggling with sinful habits as though they did not truly get saved.

Through years of experience, I can testify that when we accept Christ into our hearts and lives, the Lord's Spirit begins a work of Grace in us to conform us to the image of Christ. This transformation is a gradual process, not an overnight change. It's a journey of patience, hope, and understanding. Delivering some of us from past hurts and bad habits can take a lifetime. Let's be patient and understanding, knowing everyone's spiritual journey is unique and takes time. God, who is patient and rich in mercy, will guide us through this growing process, helping develop our character and causing us to become more like him; it's essential to understand that even after accepting the gift of salvation, our minds, influenced and tainted by the impurities present in the world, continue to harbor resistance against God's ways.

Our minds are conditioned to think in ways contrary to God's will, making it difficult for us to align ourselves with His will. We must renew our minds daily by reading and meditating on God's word to overcome this. Spending time with God in prayer is essential as it helps us connect with Him intimately and understand His will for our lives. By changing our thought patterns, focusing on positive influences, and strengthening our relationship with God through prayer, meditation, and reflection on spiritual teachings, we can effectively counteract and rise above the harmful impact of the world's negativity and live a life that is pleasing to Him.

I encourage you to read and engage with this book's contents. By embracing and applying its principles, you will embark on a journey of personal growth within your Christian faith, deepen your connection with God, and gain a profound comprehension of His extraordinary grace.

Upon reading this book, we hope you will be persuaded that regardless of the challenges life presents, you can take comfort in knowing that a wonderful power creator has intricately planned and orchestrated every aspect of your life from its inception to its culmination. (Jeremiah 29:11)

(Jeremiah 29:11) "For I know the thoughts that I think toward you, saith the LORD, thoughts of peace, and not of evil, to give you an expected end."

CHAPTER 1

BREAKING OLD HABITS

Have you ever encountered people who believe their salvation experience with Christ was a complete deliverance moment, where all their sins and bad habits were immediately removed? Such people often testify that they experienced a profound change and now live a sin-free life, free from any addictions or harmful habits. They believe such a transformation is the hallmark of true salvation, and people are not genuinely saved if they are still struggling with bad habits and strongholds. This belief has been debated among Christians, with some arguing that it's not a one-size-fits-all situation. They believe, and I think from experience, that I can agree with them that sanctification is a journey. It's not unusual for a believer to experience struggles with sin and bad habits. It's not the absence of sin that defines true salvation but rather the presence of Christ in one's life.

May I ask if you have had a salvation experience where all your sins and bad habits were immediately removed, or have you been sanctified? Please know that I am not putting these leaders or their beliefs down. Still, I am stating that the enemy may use their beliefs and teaching to create doubt and even deter those who may not have been brought up in church or have even heard about God until they heard the gospel message preached under the anointing of a dear Saint of God.

I can testify to the transformative power of God's love in the lives of new converts. Even those once rejected by a church body have experienced a profound change. Some of these precious people may have lived lives that were not in line with God's teachings, but after surrendering to the Lord, they began to noticc a shift in their behavior, likes, and desires. This is a testament to the incredible power of God's love to bring about spiritual transformation.

I remember when one guy continued playing music in the bars with his band. Still, the desire to play in this environment began to weigh heavily on him, causing him to feel that what he was doing was wrong and that he was in the wrong climate using his gift. Did you know that the discomfort grew so strong in the man that he could not shake it, and over time, it became evident that he loved his church and pastor more than his desire to play worldly music? The man discovered that when he approached his pastor about the situation, he received great wisdom and was informed that using his gift in that environment was not bringing God glory. The pastor told him that the precious Spirit of God, who was now operating inside of him, was grieved when he entered the entertainment places in the world. Did you know that man began to study God's word for himself and discover God's commands for Christian living, finding out what God likes and dislikes, including what his word says about the "shall and shall not," which can bring a curse or a blessing?

Beloved, his pastor, informed him that God's Spirit had begun a work in his life, and he would be the one to finish it through his work of Grace. Please know that when we surrender our lives to the Lord (through salvation) and ask him into our hearts, he immediately takes us at our word, and our Spirit is given life. After we receive Christ into our hearts and lives, our mind is still an enemy to the things of God and must be renewed by spending time in his word daily. When dealing with new converts, please know that they may have never been in church before and do not know what is contrary to God's word because of their moral upbringing, or maybe they have never been to church or in an environment where the gospel or expression of God's love was shared, therefore beloved, we cannot expect a new Christian to know what we know. Remember, the saying goes, "Do not throw the baby out with the bath water." The essence of this message is that new Christians may not know or understand that something they are doing is wrong. But our wonderful and loving heavenly Father works in them through his Spirit to convict them and make them aware that something is amiss in their surroundings. God's Spirit is there to convict (convince), not condemn them, that something is out of line from his righteous will. This assurance of God's Spirit's guidance is a source of comfort and support for new Christians, reminding them that they are not alone in their faith journey. God takes them seriously when they ask him to make their life count for his glory, and he will work with their faults and ignorance to bring them into the plan and purpose he has for their life.

We can rest assured that just like the parable that declares he left the ninety-and-nine to go after the one that went astray, God's Holy Spirit will continually work patiently with them to bring them to his will, even encouraging them to seek advice from a pastor, or he may even lead them to study his word and find out for themselves what he likes and dislikes. God has a plan for every life born on this planet, and who knows, they may have a precious, dear mother praying, using words such as, "Dear Lord, please push back the evil from my child and place some of your people in their path who truly love you that may show them the way to their deliverance." When individuals discover the reason behind their emotions, they will appreciate the Lord for giving them the fullness of his grace. This will inspire them to share their faith with other band members, explaining the new-found joy and peace they have found in Christ. As a result, they may inform their fellow band members that they can no longer perform music in the bar scene. Have you ever witnessed the transformation that occurs when someone hears the good news of the gospel? It's truly remarkable. A veil is lifted from their eyes when they learn that God knew everything about them before they were born. They realize that they no longer have to carry the weight of their mistakes and failures and that their struggles were known to God from the beginning. This revelation brings them an incredible sense of peace and freedom. They begin to see their life in a new light, no longer filled with confusion and aimlessness. They start to believe that they have a purpose and a destiny and that God has a plan for their life.

Their hope is renewed, and they find the strength to face each day with courage and determination. It's as if the gospel has unlocked a door they never knew existed, and they step into a new world of possibility and potential. It's a beautiful thing to witness and a reminder of the power of God's love to transform lives. It's interesting to note that the same holds for cohabiting couples. When they are faced with the decision of whether or not to engage in sexual activity, they may feel a sense of conviction in their heart and begin to make plans to get married, or they may choose to move out and refrain from any sexual relations with their partner until they are officially married. Many factors, such as personal beliefs, cultural norms, and societal expectations, can influence this decision. Ultimately, what matters most is that both partners feel comfortable and respected in their choices regarding their relationship and plans. As believers, it is essential to remember that when someone becomes a new Christian, they will likely make mistakes and stumble along the way. The process of learning and growing in faith is a journey, and it is not uncommon for new believers to struggle with certain aspects of their newfound faith. It is crucial to recognize that during this time, the devil will quickly pounce on any opportunity to condemn and discourage these new believers. He will use his tricks to convince them they have gone too far or done something unforgivable.

In closing this chapter, let me say that according to the Bible, our Creator designed the first Adam to be perfect until he fell into sin. Man fell into sin when satan succeeded in convincing Eve that God was withholding something from them, which led her to take the forbidden fruit from the Tree of Knowledge. Adam, who was with her, also ate the fruit. Deceiving Eve in the garden made it easy for satan to lead them astray. The message portrayed throughout this chapter teaches us about the power of temptation and the consequences that follow when we give in to it. It also emphasizes the significance of free will and the responsibility that comes with it. As human beings, we possess the unique ability to exercise our free will.

We can make choices that significantly impact our lives. For instance, we can climb a tower and jump off it. However, the moment we make that decision, we relinquish control, and the laws of physics take over. We are subject to the force of gravity, which pulls us down, resulting in severe injury or even death upon impact. Similarly, when we live in a way that goes against God's word, we open ourselves up to the traps set by an enemy who doesn't have our best interests at heart. The enemy may tempt us with temporary pleasures, leading to destruction and misery. In contrast, living according to God's principles brings us peace, joy, and fulfillment. It is up to us to make choices that align with God's will and protect us from the dangers of the enemy's traps.

CHAPTER 2

CAN I STILL LIVE IN SIN?

In today's modern world, people are becoming increasingly self-centered. They are always in a hurry, moving from one task to another but ultimately getting nowhere. This leaves little time for reflection or self-examination. As a result, many individuals are losing touch with their spiritual selves and becoming more focused on their desires and needs. Did you not know that this shift from a God-centered perspective to self-centeredness can significantly affect our society?

The word of God tells us that at the beginning of creation, humanity's nature that our Creator designed was called "very good," which means that man's nature was not created evil, but it became evil through the influence of Satan who was able to convince Eve that God was holding something back from them. Once Satan had deceived the woman, it was easy to get them to eat the forbidden fruit. Once they committed this willful act, sin entered the garden, which tells us that Adam and Eve were given one law to keep. They failed miserably in keeping that one law, but God, in his foreknowledge, knew that they would not be able to keep that law, and does not the scriptures tell us that "Jesus was slain before the foundation of the world?" (Revelation 13:8)

When we read our bible, we will discover that by the second generation of man, murder had occurred when Cain killed his brother Abel in a heated rage, and did you know that man was so very corrupt during the time of the flood that God had to intervene to bring judgment to his creation, and did you know that the same evil influences that lead to the moral deterioration of society are still evident in the world today, and did you know that every person born into the world is exposed to the same spirits and temptations that influenced Adam and Eve?

Below are some scriptures the unidentified man, whom I believe was an Angel of the Lord, mentioned to me when I thought I had messed up. Yes, I believe he was an Angel, especially after vanishing in plain sight while walking away from me.

During an interview with KROV Radio and All Nations TV in San Antonio, Texas, I was asked what God had done for me over the years. I replied, "He has scared the devil out of me, and I was not exaggerating."

(Romans 7:14-16) (14) "For we know that the law is spiritual: but I am carnal, sold under sin." (15) "For that which I do I allow not: for what I would, that do I not; but what I hate, that do I." (16) "If then I do that which I would not, I consent unto the law that it is good." (Romans 7:17-18) (17) "Now then it is no more I that do it, but sin that dwelleth in me." (18) "For I know that in me (that is, in my flesh,) dwelleth no good thing: for to will is present with me, but how to perform that which is good I find not."

(Romans 7:19 -21) (19) "For the good that I would I do not: but the evil which I would not, that I do." (20) "Now if I do that I would not, it is no more I that do it, but sin that dwelleth in me." (21) "I find then a law, that, when I would do good, evil is present with me."

(Romans 7:22 -24) (22) "For I delight in the law of God after the inward man:" (23) "But I see another law in my members, warring against the law of my mind, and bringing me into captivity to the law of sin which is in my members." (24) "O wretched man that I am! who shall deliver me from the body of this death?"

(Galatians 2:20) "I am crucified with Christ: nevertheless, I live; yet not I, but Christ liveth in me: and the life which I now live in the flesh I live by the faith of the Son of God, who loved me and gave himself for me."

By the leading of God's Spirit, I will now open up a revelation of what the Apostle Paul was stating in these remarkable passages above, and we can better understand what Paul is speaking about by using the illustration of having two dogs in our presence. Let's say that one of the dogs is leaner than the other for lack of nourishment, and will not common sense tell us that the one we feed the most will be stronger than the other? Therefore, if we keep feeding the undernourished dog, he will also gain weight and grow, possibly even outgrow the other dog.

Paul is making a statement in (Galatians 2:20) something like there is something in him that causes him to do things that he does not want to do, which he is referring to the sinful nature that was passed down through the blood of Adam.

(Galatians 2:20)"I am crucified with Christ; nevertheless, I live; yet not I, but Christ liveth in me: and the life which I now live in the flesh I live by the faith of the Son of God, who loved me and gave himself for me."

Therefore, Paul tells us that he sincerely desires to please God, but sometimes, that old, sinful nature gets in his way. Through these verses, he shows us the warfare taking place within his soul, as the flesh man with his fleshly desire wars against the spirit man who rejects the cravings of the flesh.

Like many of us, the Apostle Paul said he desires to live a crucified life but has a problem. That problem is that he is still alive in the flesh. He still has those ugly fleshly desires to contend with, but notice, beloved, that he gives us his secret to being an overcomer, and that secret is trusting in the work God is doing in his life through the indwelling presence of his Holy Spirit.

(Romans 7:21) "When I would do good, evil is present with me," and notice in (Romans 7:24) where he asks an important question, "O wretched man that I am! Who shall deliver me from the body of this death?"

During the mid-1980s through 1994, I experienced a seven-year plus nervous breakdown. During that time, I met an elderly gentleman I believe to have been an Angel of the Lord. This meeting occurred at a truck stop, profoundly impacting my life. That night before meeting him, I became weak and gave in to temptation, and the following day, I found myself feeling betrayed, used, and abused.

This led me to carry the weight of condemnation from that act into a truck-stop restaurant. While having breakfast, I thought that if I ever had any connection with God, it was long gone. As I left, an elderly gentleman held the door for me and asked to speak with me outside. I agreed to meet the man outside the establishment, and to my surprise, he told me that God loved me enough to send him to minister to me that morning. This was the second Angel God sent me since I started living like the world. I know it got my full attention, and I often think of it even now while ministering in other countries. The man I now believe was an Angel began informing me that God loved me and had a great ministry waiting on me, but beloved; what he said next made me realize that someone had been watching my every move, even behind closed doors! The older man stated that just because you mess up with a member of the opposite flesh, it does not cancel God's plan in your life and stop the world from turning. The man's face began to shine like the sun as he quoted these verses from (Romans 7:24) emphasizing the twenty-fourth verse, which asks, "Who shall deliver me from the body of this death?"

During our conversation, the man shifted the topic and started describing the beauty of Heaven. He expressed his belief that my current assignment on Earth is to become a powerful minister that God will use to change many lives. He also mentioned that according to what he had been shown, God has already seen me cross the finish line and enter His Heaven."

I want you to know that after informing me that the Lord God Jehovah sent him to me, someone yelled at me, and as I turned to look, the man started walking away and vanished in thin air right before my very eyes. I remember those seven long years trying to discover myself by driving those 18-wheel trucks in an attempt to outrun my troubled past, and I still remember placing that gun under my chin to end my life while parked beside the Associations of Christian Truckers Chapel that was located in the truck stop in Carlisle Pennsylvania. I also remember the pretty redhead lady chaplain named Kris Tackitt and her well-built Navy husband named Joe, who had the words I needed to hear concerning the flesh, which caused me to make it a point to stop by when my trips to the East Coast brought me their way which was usually every other week.

I wanted to know how a so-called man of God could rape their daughters, including going with anything wearing a skirt, and still stand in a church and preach? Chaplain Kris, wearing her white Go-Go boots, replied, "Honey, it is because the flesh wants to do what it loves and knows how to do, and some of these ministers in their younger years have probably been abused too."

She went on to use the passage of scripture found in (1 Samuel 15:32-33), speaking of Samuel instructing King Saul to carry out God's command to destroy the Amalekites, a rebellious kingdom that had long defied God's will. According to the text, God had ordered Saul to destroy everything living in the kingdom, including the animals, as a punishment for the Amalekites' rebellion.

She said, "When Saul and his army conquered the Amalekites, he spared the life of King Agag, the Amalekite king." He kept the best animals alive, possibly intending to offer them as a sacrifice to the Lord. This action of sparing King Agag and the best animals went against God's command and angered Samuel. When Samuel confronted Saul about this disobedience, Saul claimed he had kept the animals alive to offer them sacrifices to God. However, Samuel rebuked Saul, stating that obeying God's commands was more important than offering sacrifices. She said, "The scriptures highlight the importance of obedience to God's commands and the consequences of disobedience, reminding us to always put our faith in God and trust in His will, even when we do not fully understand it.

(1 Samuel 15:32-33) (32) "Then said Samuel, Bring ye hither to me Agag the king of the Amalekites. And Agag came unto him delicately. And Agag said, Surely the bitterness of death is past." (33) "And Samuel said, as thy sword hath made women childless, so shall thy mother be childless among women. And Samuel hewed Agag in pieces before the LORD in Gilgal."

The woman chaplain stressed that the Prophet Samuel instructed King Saul not to allow anything to live in the kingdom of Agag and not to touch or covet any of the spoil. Still, King Saul listened to the people's cries instead of God's commands, which caused God to reject him as the King of Israel.

The lady chaplain said, "We can look at this story and liken King Agag to a type of the flesh, and you know what happened in the end: the prophet Samuel took a sword and slew the king, and we must do the same to the temptations of our flesh, especially if we are going to be successful in our Christian Walk here on earth."

Did you know that under the reign of the Roman Empire, if a man was convicted of taking the life of another man, the dead man was tied to him? He was forced to live in the valley of Gehenna, often called the valley of fire, because this beloved was where all trash and discarded pottery were cast to eliminate the unwanted junk.

Did you know that this valley is where it is believed that Judas, who betrayed Jesus, hung himself? To this day, this area is called the Valley of Discarded Pottery. Did you know that if pottery had a flaw, there was nothing they could do to rework the clay that would take out the flaw? They discovered that if they visited a Shepard and found a specific tick that had been sucking the blood of one of their lambs that when they would mix the blood from the tick, which represents the world, and the blood from the lamb into the flawed pottery, the pottery would go back together without a flaw?

Did you know that the man who was sentenced to live his life here in this valley of Gehenna with the punishment of having the corpse tied on his back is to live in this valley till the corpse rotted off, which meant that the diseases and skin worms from that corpse would significantly impact his body?

Did you know that this meant that if the man could find water or food, he had no choice but to drink and eat with the dead man tied to his body? This is a type of our outward flesh tied to us, and no matter how often we may think we have our flesh buried, we are still human. When someone or something out of the norm pushes us beyond our limits, we will sometimes discover that our old human nature attempts to resurrect, and when we go to get a drink of water, the old man will try to get one with us.

Paul's desire to live the crucified life is a journey we all share. He acknowledges the struggle of living in the flesh with its earthly lusts, but he also understands that victory is possible. The key is to submit ourselves to the guidance and leadership of God's blessed Holy Spirit. As the Apostle Paul cries out through these scriptures, "Who shall deliver me from the power of this death?" We, too, can find hope in the Holy Spirit's power to guide us.

Notice how the Apostle Paul gets hopeful when he realizes that only God can help us overcome the flesh if we give the battle to him. Did you know that when we feed the spirit man with God's word and spend quality time with him in prayer, we will discover that the spirit man part of us will be more decisive, giving us more power to bring the flesh under control?

Studying the scriptures listed in our references, we will discover that Paul is letting us know that every time he desires to live the crucified life by keeping the flesh with its desires put under submission and buried, there are times when he discovers that the older man is attempting to be resurrected.

The bottom line to this message lies in the fact that the Apostle not only realized that he was still alive in the flesh, but he realized that he could be his own worst enemy. If we look at (Galatians 2:20), we will find that Paul reveals to us that he can draw strength in knowing that what he cannot do in this walk of faith because of being weak in the flesh, God's Spirit will do through him.

(Galatians 2:20) "I am crucified with Christ: nevertheless, I live; yet not I, but Christ liveth in me: and the life which I now live in the flesh I live by the faith of the Son of God, who loved me and gave himself for me."

Dear reader, (John 15:16) gives us a picture of the call and plan of God for our life, which occurred before the foundation of the world, and we understand that it is in Christ that we live and have our being. (Acts 17:28)

The essence of life itself is summarized in the divine presence of Christ. His teachings on love, compassion, and forgiveness embody the core values that guide us through our journey on earth. Christ's message of hope and salvation resonates deeply with believers, offering them strength, peace, and purpose. The impact of Christ's life and teachings extends beyond the individual level, shaping entire communities and cultures for millennia. In Him, we live and have our being; therefore, let us strive for perfection and enter into God's rest.

God speaks volumes in the fifteen chapters of John's gospel and the sixteenth verse that he called us and ordained us that we should go forth and bring forth fruit and that our fruit should remain; that whatsoever we shall ask of the Father in his name, he may give it unto us. The scriptures we just reviewed plainly state that God is the one who chose us; therefore, it is up to him to finish the work, and all that is required on our part is to be willing to surrender our life to him and abide in his amazing grace and unchanging love. The grace we have received is not a result of our efforts but a gift from God's Spirit actively working in our lives. This grace, freely given to us, is continually upheld and nurtured by the guiding force of God's Spirit.

The scriptures assure us that the church of God will be presented on that particular day as spotless and without blemish. This presentation will be possible only because of the work of God's Spirit in the lives of believers.

The scriptures highlight the importance of God's grace and the role of His Spirit in initiating and completing this work of grace in our lives. It also emphasizes the ultimate goal of this work of grace, which is to present us, His church, as spotless and without a blemish on the day when Christ returns to claim us as His bride; we can rejoice in knowing that "The Holy Spirit who is equipped with the divine plans that God has for our lives has descended to guide us into all truth and righteousness, for the glory of His name."

CHAPTER 3
WHAT IF I SHOULD FALL?

Let's clarify that the title of this chapter is not a question of "What if I should fall," but "What do I do when I fall?" Beloved, sooner or later, we will mess up, and did you know that sometimes, our loving God will put us in a place where we cannot win? God is more interested in us learning the lesson through the test, which will help cultivate the character he is looking for because he is more interested in character than in us passing the test. The word says that all have fallen and have come short of the glory of God, which is in Christ Jesus, and I have noticed in my Christian Walk that sometimes, God will place us in a natural situation to build character in our life. Did you not know that we are spirit beings having a human experience, and did you know that God desires for us to learn just how dangerous sin is and he desires for us to understand what it is like to love and be loved, for we are discovering what it is like to be hurt, rejected, and abused? As a beloved child of God, we must understand that he has a unique plan for each of us. He places people and opportunities in our path to help us fulfill that plan and accomplish our life purpose. Whether it is a chance encounter with a stranger or a fortuitous job opportunity, every experience can be seen as a part of God's plan.

As we navigate life, we can trust that God is working everything together for our good, even when we cannot see the bigger picture. So, let us continue to seek his guidance and trust in his providence, knowing that he is always with us every step of the way. Our God is a loving, forgiving Father. Although people may be unforgiving, we can rest in knowing that our God, in his foreknowledge, knew how we were going to mess up and chose to call us anyway, for what the enemy doesn't want us to know is that our God has already made provision for all our sins past, present, and future, for when they were placed on Jesus at the cross; his death satisfied the wrath of a sin-hating God bridging the gap back to God that lost through the fall of Adam. Did you know that God's law against sin was so binding that it placed Jesus on the cross to die in our place; have you not read where the word of God says, "He that knew no sin was made sin for us and that while we were yet sinners, Christ died for us?" (2 Corinthians 5:21)

Jesus (the other Adam) had to be tried as a criminal and convicted; He then had to be executed as a convicted criminal, for our redeemer had to be another Adam with God's original blood and not the blood from man to pay the sin debt against humanity. God did not desire to make another Adam from the dust of the earth like he did Adam because the planet was now under a curse, and did not the scriptures declare that in the fullness of time, God made himself a body and placed it in the Virgin Mary to bring forth a Savior into the world.

The word states that “God was in Christ reconciling the world back to himself,” or in other words, God was attempting to rescue as many as possible of his most incredible creation from the rebellion of Satan. We are going to make mistakes, and yes, we are going to fall, but we have some hope that is found in the word of God that says, “The just man falleth seven times and riseth again, which means that he will always get back up.” (Proverbs 24:16)

Did you know that the Christian life is a learning process, and we need to know that when we mess up, we can come to our Heavenly Father and fall on his available and rich mercy to all who call upon his name?

I want to emphasize an essential message for all the believers out there. As we go through our lives, we are bound to make mistakes and experience failures. However, we must remember that we don't need to hide from God as Adam and Eve did in the garden when they sinned. Instead, we should run towards Him with open arms, knowing He is a merciful and loving God who is always ready to restore us. Our Heavenly Father is a restorer to those who turn to Him. He is not here to condemn us but to guide us toward the right path, help us learn from our mistakes, and become better individuals. God's love and mercy are infinite, and He is always ready to forgive us, no matter how many times we fall. We must trust in His goodness and turn to Him with a humble heart, seeking His forgiveness and guidance. His love and mercy are our secure refuge, a comforting assurance that we are never alone in our journey.

Let us always remember that we have a Father in Heaven who loves us unconditionally and is always ready to restore us when we go astray. Let us seek His forgiveness and guidance whenever we stumble and trust in His goodness and mercy, remembering that God sees in the light, and he sees clearly in the dark; therefore, he knows what we have done and what we are going to do because although the scriptures teach that he knows the end from the beginning, he is more interested in character. God knows what he wants. It is okay to miss the mark in target practice as it would be to mess up in a real battle. God fore-knew we were going to mess up but decided to call us anyway, and no matter how bad we may have messed up or how far away we may feel from him, there is joy in knowing that we can run to the safety of his open arms, knowing he will not turn us away. We are his children, and he is the one that began the work of grace in us, and he will be the one that will finish the work that we may be presented on that day blameless and without spot or shame.

Did you not know that we are spirit beings having a human experience that we may learn what it is like to love and be loved; we are discovering what it is like to be hurt, rejected, and abused because the bottom line would be that we are also discovering how evil sin is and the reason God set moral laws in place? Did you know that God knows his plans for each of his children and places people and things in our path to help steer us toward fulfilling that plan?

It is written in the Scripture that all of us have sinned and fallen short of the glory of God, which is found in Christ Jesus. Every human has made mistakes and fallen short of God's perfect standard. As a believer in Christ, I have realized that sometimes God allows us to face situations where we are likely to succeed, not to make us proud or arrogant but to build our character and help us grow in our faith. These natural-win situations can be seen as opportunities to develop skills, build confidence, and increase our faith in God. These situations teach us to trust God more and rely on Him for strength and guidance. We also learn to be grateful for His blessings and to use them to serve others and bring glory to His name.

Meeting those Angels helped open my eyes to a loving God who is not looking for me to fall, but God sent his Angel to help me understand that when I mess up, his grace will help me overcome it. We know and have heard of Christian leaders today who have fallen and brought a mark against the Kingdom of God, but does God throw them away because of their weakness? The answer is a resounding NO! Our God is a loving, forgiving Father, and although people may be unforgiving, we can rest in knowing that our God, in his foreknowledge, knew how we would mess up and called us anyway. What the enemy doesn't want us to know is that God has already made provision for all our sins, past, present, and future, for when they were placed on Jesus at the cross, his death satisfied the wrath of a sin-hating God.

Jesus (the other Adam) had to be tried as a criminal and convicted; He then had to be executed as a convicted criminal. Our redeemer had to be another Adam with God's original blood and not the blood of man to pay the sinful debt against humanity. God didn't desire to make another Adam from the dust of the earth like he did Adam because the planet, after the fall, was placed under a curse. The scriptures declare that in the fullness of time, God made himself a body and put it in the Virgin Mary to bring forth a Savior into the world. According to the Bible, God was present in Christ, working towards reconciling the world to himself. This means that God was trying to save as many people as possible from Satan's rebellion.

Let's remember that God, in his infinite wisdom, allowed his Son, Christ Jesus, to endure pain and punishment so he would not have to punish man, his most significant creation. We are bound to make mistakes, and yes, we will fall, but we have unwavering hope in the word of God that says, "The just man falleth seven times, but he will always get back up." This is a message of reassurance, a reminder that the Christian life is a learning process, and when we stumble, we can always turn to our Heavenly Father and fall on his mercy, which is available to all who call upon his name. The central idea of this message is that people are bound to make mistakes and fall short of their expectations. However, when we do, we should not feel discouraged or run away from God; instead, we should remember that He is always there for us.

In the Holy Bible, we learn that when Adam and Eve sinned, they hid from God, but in reality, God was seeking them out. Similarly, we should turn to God and seek His guidance and forgiveness when we make mistakes. The Bible tells us that God is near to those who have a contrite heart and a humble spirit. This means that when we come to God with a repentant heart and a willingness to change, He is always ready to forgive and guide us on the right path. His guidance is not distant or impersonal but a loving and personal journey with each of us.

Now, let's do a deep, thought-provoking study of the Parable of the Sower from the Bible, a significant narrative found in the book of Matthew, particularly in chapter thirteen. This parable, with its seeds symbolizing the word of God and the various types of soil representing the diverse ways people receive and respond to this word, holds immense relevance in our journey of spiritual growth. Some seeds fell by the wayside, and the birds quickly devoured them. Other seeds fell on stony ground, where they sprang up quickly, but the sun scorched them and withered away because they had no soil depth. Some seeds fell among thorns, and the thorns grew up and choked them. Finally, some seeds fell on good soil and produced a bountiful harvest, yielding a hundred, sixty, or thirty times what was sown. This parable teaches us how people receive and respond to the word of God, and it invites us to reflect deeply on our receptivity and response to God's word in our lives. This reflection is a crucial part of our spiritual journey, encouraging us to be introspective and contemplative.

Throughout the ministry the Lord entrusted unto me, I have witnessed people having spiritual encounters and undergoing significant transformations. Most of these divine encounters and transformations occurred when individuals felt a deep connection with God, often accompanied by a profound sense of peace, joy, or understanding. Various experiences, such as a powerful sermon, a personal revelation, or a moment of prayer, can trigger these moments. These experiences often result in significant changes in the individual's beliefs, attitudes, and behaviors. It is remarkable to see individuals gain new perspectives on morality and ethics and then dedicate themselves to sharing their journeys. Your role in sharing the profound message of God's love and redemption is integral to our community and is deeply valued. I have witnessed individuals express their faith wholeheartedly and guide others to the Lord. I have also witnessed people wrestle with moments of weakness in their faith, especially when confronted with temptations and trials that seem to gnaw at their souls. Some of these people have regrettably lapsed back into behaviors of sin, yielding to old temptations. This has led me to ponder the root cause of their relapse. Could it be attributed to a lack of support, the lingering effect of generational curses, or perhaps unresolved personal issues? The Holy Bible reminds us that the human heart is always inclined towards evil. This underscores the crucial role of mutual accountability in upholding righteousness and moral conduct.

To foster this, many congregations have established follow-up ministry initiatives. These initiatives, including having regular small group meetings for accountability and support, one-on-one mentorship programs, and educational resources to deepen understanding of the faith, are vital in providing the support, mentorship, and direction we need to navigate and strengthen our spiritual journeys.

In our discussions and gatherings, I find it crucial to reach out to individuals who may have previously been more dedicated to their Christian faith but have drifted away or become disheartened. I often refer to the scripture that advises those who have fallen from grace to return to their initial enthusiasm and commitment. I love to emphasize that their lapse in faith does not spell the end of their spiritual journey; rather, it represents a hopeful opportunity for more profound personal growth and spiritual development. This growth often begins with personal reflection and self-awareness, but it also requires the guidance and support of a mentor or guide. They haven't lost ground; instead, they have gained valuable insights that will better equip them for the road ahead, enabling them to withstand temptations and reinforcing their resolve to spread the message of God. Once you experience God's unending and incredible grace, you understand that God is brimming with compassion for every part of His creation. God’s love is not a fleeting emotion but a steadfast commitment to our well-being and growth. It dawns on you that He isn't eagerly anticipating your failures but observing and hoping for you to display maturity in your character.

This realization leads to a deepened respect and awe for Him and an increased understanding of His significance in your life. It equips you with the ability to effectively introduce Him to others as you comprehend what He has accomplished in your life and what He is capable of doing in the lives of others. His redemption is not just a one-time event but a continuous process of transformation and renewal; this understanding can guide us in our spiritual journeys.

The truth is that if the Lord had placed me in the position I currently have as an international evangelist working in ministry in another country several years ago, I believe I would not have possessed the necessary maturity, experience, and wisdom to fulfill the responsibilities that come with this position effectively. I have come to understand that my growth and development, both personally and spiritually, have equipped me to handle this role with greater confidence and capability.

In summary, I vividly recall a moment of prayer around 3:00 a.m. one morning. I humbly expressed remorse to my heavenly father for the squandered time and years marred by continual errors in my past. During this intimate exchange, I distinctly heard his voice interjecting my prayers, reassuring me with the words, "My child, if you had not endured those trials back then, you would not possess the wisdom needed to fulfill your current purpose."

We must remember that God's love and grace are always available to us, no matter how big or small our mistakes may be. We should not be afraid to come to Him with our brokenness and trust in His unfailing love and mercy. God's love demonstrated his mercy in giving his Son Jesus to die in our place. My dear friend, the mercy of God is a profound and wondrous thing. We are reminded of this mercy every time we contemplate the old, rugged cross upon which Jesus Christ, the Son of God, gave his life for us. Through his sacrifice, we can experience the fullness of God's mercy. As we gather for worship, it is essential to remember that everything we do—from our songs and prayers to our preaching and giving—should reflect God's mercy. We should be grateful for Jesus's sacrifice and strive to live our lives in a way that honors it. Let us never forget God's mercy, made visible through Jesus Christ.

Our God, who sits on his throne and oversees all of creation, is unmatched in his power and glory. He is beloved by all for his ability to judge and rule fairly and justly. Notably, our mighty God is not threatened by warring spirits or forces attempting to overthrow him. This is because he is all-powerful and majestic, and his rule over all creation is unchallenged. We are reminded of his immense power and glory as we approach him, and we can take comfort in knowing he is watching over us and guiding us toward the right path. Having faith in this divine creator and seeking his guidance in all aspects of our lives is crucial to living an abundant life.

With his help, we can overcome obstacles and achieve our goals, knowing we are under his protection and care. I want to remind you of God's incredible love for us. He created us in His image and has a unique plan for each of us. It's hard to fathom that the same God who created the universe cares so deeply for us, but it's true. He desires to have a relationship with us and to guide us through this life. I pray that as you read this message, you will feel a sense of hunger to know God more intimately. He is the one who loved us so much that He made a way to deliver us from our sins. His sacrifice on the cross is the ultimate expression of love and should inspire us to draw closer to Him. When we spend time in God's presence, we are transformed. We become more like Him, and our desires align with His will. It's beautiful to walk in step with Him, and I pray you will experience this more sincerely today. God loves you more than you could ever imagine. His plan for your life is good, and He desires to walk with you every step of the way.

CHAPTER 4
GROWING IN GRACE

I begin this chapter by emphasizing that saved people are adopted into God's family as his children, and God does not have any grownups in this walk of faith, nor does he have grandchildren, for we are all being changed and conformed daily into the image of his dear Son. Did you know that some individuals tend to grow and mature more spiritually than others who have gone through similar experiences? When someone has undergone a difficult period, they may emerge from it with a greater understanding of themselves and the world around them. This understanding often leads to a more profound spiritual growth, which sets them apart from others who have been through the same trials. These individuals are frequently referred to as elders and are held in high esteem by their community members.

Did you know that we are often placed in situations that will try our faith and stretch us sometimes to our breaking point? Did you know that the trial of our faith can be likened to meat processing? If we knew how some of our meat was processed, would we throw it away and not consume it? Preparing meat for sale in the meat industry can be pretty complicated. Sometimes, it involves mixing the meat with substances that may not appeal to the taste or smell. Beloved, this process is necessary to ensure that the meat meets the required sales standards.

All of our life's good and bad encounters are carefully planned to give us the necessary training to mature and fulfill the assignment planned for us before the world began. New converts must find a good Bible-believing church and attend meetings as often as possible. This provides them with the support and encouragement to navigate their newfound faith. In the face of the challenges, we must unite and build our spirits to resist the devil's daily attacks. We need each other to face these challenges and build a strong foundation of faith. It's interesting to note that the presence of God's anointing can vary depending on the situation. For instance, when we gather together to worship, there are times when we can feel the anointing of God more strongly than when we are on our own. The power of God's blessing can be tangible when we unite as a community of believers, and that's why attending church regularly and being part of a community focused on building a solid relationship with God is essential. When we worship with our fellow believers, we can experience the fullness of God's anointing and be transformed by His power. Did you know that a true leader will always show love, keep an open mind, and remain teachable, eager to gain greater wisdom in the things of God? This level of humility and submission doesn't happen overnight. We need each other for the coming trials, and we must build up our spirits to face the devil's daily onslaughts. Did you know that there is a different presence of God's anointing in a collective body, such as a church, not to be found in our prayer closet?

Dear reader, can you imagine meeting someone who has been to England, and instead of speaking about the splendors found in the country, they come back talking about the mouse under the Queen's chair?

The truth is, "there will always be fault finders in a church body," and the perfect church without fault or blame will not be found in a fallen world with imperfect people. But does not the word of God teach that we are being renewed day by day? This concept of renewal should fill us with hope and encouragement, knowing that we are not defined by our past mistakes but by our continuous growth and renewal in God's grace.

As we conclude this chapter, I advise new converts that studying and learning from the church's teachings is essential for their Christian growth. This will help you to build a strong foundation of faith. After a few years of learning, you can approach the pastor and humbly seek guidance on strengthening further and demonstrating your faith. By doing so, you show your commitment to growth and seek to align yourself with the pastor's vision for the congregation. Continue to set aside a specific time to be in solitude with God, and he will look forward to meeting you to show you things that may affect you or a member of your family; remember that God wants us to come to him broken in spirit and confess our sins to him, who will forgive us and cleanse us from all unrighteousness.

If we try and cover up our sins and continue therein, God will expose and embarrass us, for he loves us too much to leave us to our demise because he would rather have us embarrassed than lose us to Satan only to end up in eternity without him. God's love for us and desire for our growth in his kingdom is unwavering. He promised never to leave and always be with us until the world's end. Therefore, we should remember that No matter what kinds of difficulties we encounter in life, whether they involve emotional pain such as heartache or deep sadness, it's essential to recognize that there is always a meaningful purpose behind these experiences. God always works behind the scenes to ensure everything turns out according to his plan and purpose. The more we mature in the things of God, the more we will discover that our God is longsuffering and slow to anger, not willing that anyone would perish; therefore, did you know that God's great love towards us, his most incredible creation is an everlasting, unchanging love that reaches to the highest heaven and descends to the lowest hell, therefore, may we rejoice in knowing that we are a purchased possession that Christ purchased with his blood? May we ever be thankful for his redeeming love that made us be adopted into his family as Sons and Daughters in his kingdom; therefore, in closing this paragraph, may we find some consolation in knowing that (Isaiah 49:16) states that God has our names engraved on the palms of his hands.

CHAPTER 5

DISCOVERING YOUR PURPOSE IN LIFE

I begin this chapter with an urgency to have you understand that we are all born with a unique and meaningful purpose in life, and it is our responsibility to discover and fulfill that purpose. Each of us has a destiny waiting to be fulfilled, and it is through our actions and choices, we strive to reach our full potential and positively impact the world around us. As some people may think, our future is not a short time ahead of us, but in reality, it lies within us, as it was placed in us at birth by a wonderful and loving Creator. Our destinies are not predetermined by time; from the moment of our birth, they are intricately woven into our being by a benevolent and loving Creator. Our future is hurtling toward us just as swiftly as we are hurtling toward it. Timing is crucial in God's plan, as He fully comprehends and oversees everything. God has a plan to prosper and bring us to a determined end."

(Jeremiah 29:11) "For I know the thoughts that I think toward you, saith the LORD, thoughts of peace, and not of evil, to give you an expected end."

Although we may not understand God's entire plan for our lives, there is nothing better than living Holy lives, reverently worshiping the Lord our God, and remembering that his will and purpose were placed in us at birth. Therefore, each of us prayerfully needs to search out God's plan for our lives by spending time in his word and presence. When we finally discover God's purpose for us, that purpose will help establish our vision, for vision is what God desires us to contribute toward the building of his kingdom.

God has placed his eternal purpose within our hearts, which drives us forward and motivates us to accomplish great things in his kingdom. Beloved, we were all born at a specific time in history for a reason. God has a plan for each of us, and he chose the precise moment and location for us to be born so that he could use us to leave our mark on the world. God's plan for our lives is not something we can accomplish alone. We need his help and guidance to fulfill our purpose. But the good news is that God has equipped us with everything we need to succeed. He has given us his Holy Spirit, who lives within us and empowers us to achieve his plans. When we trust in God and follow his plan for our lives, we can be confident that we will succeed. God never calls us to do something that we cannot achieve. His Spirit is within us, guiding us every step of the way and bringing his plans to fruition, which lets us know that we were born for a purpose and that God has a plan for our lives.

We must trust and allow him to guide us on our journey, and with his help, we can accomplish great things and leave a lasting legacy for future generations. Have you ever considered that we are the central players in the eternal plan of the Living God? We will only be fulfilled as Christians once we find our place and purpose within that plan. Once we understand and connect with our purpose, it will drive our vision, and we will need to pursue it with all our heart and strength. We must remind ourselves that we are valuable and deserving individuals who can achieve the dreams and goals God has placed within us for His cause and purpose.

(Ecclesiastes 3:1) "To everything there is a season, a time for every purpose under heaven."

Did you know that many people let life's difficulties give them a reason to stop living? I must admit that I have been guilty of this at times. However, when life seems to get us down, we can take cues from the sailors of the old. When a strong storm would appear out of nowhere on the open seas, they would tie themselves to the mast of the ship using some rope. This way, they would be held secure and not get washed overboard. As believers, we live in unprecedented times where danger lurks around every corner in many cities. We must strengthen our faith and rely on the promise of our Master, who never leaves us nor forsakes us. We need to remind ourselves that we are not alone in this fight. Our Master has promised to be with us every step of the way, even till the end of the world or age. His presence is our most significant source of comfort and strength.

In these uncertain times, we must hold fast to our faith and trust in the power of prayer. We must tie ourselves to our Master and remain rooted in His Word. By doing so, we can be assured of His unfailing protection and guidance. Let us continue to pray for our cities and our loved ones that they may also find comfort and strength in the promise of our Master. Let us stand firm in our faith and trust His unwavering love and protection. It's essential to remember that as we journey through life, we are bound to face opposition and trials. However, we must never forget that God is always with us and never leaves us to face these difficulties alone. He assures us that He will be our rock, refuge, and strength.

Let's take a moment to reflect on this truth and thank our Heavenly Father for His unwavering presence in our lives. Despite our challenges, we can always take comfort in God's promise to walk alongside us, guide us, and see us through to the end. Let's praise Him for His goodness and faithfulness and trust that He will continue to be our source of hope and strength in the days ahead. Please know that you do not have to allow someone to tear down your sense of self-worth because their opinion of you does not have to become a reality, and God does not expect you to allow someone to make you their trash can. Takers and users do not set limits on how much they get from you, and that is why you must learn to say no and place limits on your giving, including your time.

We have the power to listen to the hostile crowd around us, or we can choose to plug into the higher power of the Living Christ and be motivated to increase his kingdom so that no matter what, the opposition may rise against us, we are more than conquerors through him who loved us and gave himself for us.

We can operate on a battery, which may consist of what we did yesterday, or we can plug into and run off the natural power source available from the throne of God, which is an everlasting supply. I choose the latter.

Being someone who has been blessed to witness incredible miracles and have been used by God in many ways during services, I have realized the importance of recognizing and sharing our gifts with others. It is not enough to rest on our past accomplishments; we must use our talents to impact someone's life today positively. As representatives of Christ, we must uphold integrity in all we do and strive to bring out the best in others, encouraging them to reach their full potential. This is how we can add something to the Kingdom of God and make a lasting impact. We have a choice: we can either sit idly by and watch or become active participants in the Kingdom of God. Let's stand together for Christ and participate in his mission. Doing so can positively impact the people around us and fulfill God's call to serve. I hope this message inspires you to reclaim what the enemy has taken from you and discover God's purpose for your life on earth.

Please remember that God is not waiting with a backup plan in case you fail because he already knows what you will do. He guides you through your weaknesses to accomplish his will without interfering with your free will. I understand this may seem complex, but I assure you it is accurate from my experience in failing and succeeding in God's work.

I ask you to make a special place for the Lord and watch the walls of difficulties appear smaller and beloved. Please remember that God loves you, and Jesus died for you so that you might live and become part of his royal family, which is recognized as sons and daughters in Christ. Amen.

(Psalms 113:7-8) (7) "He raiseth up the poor out of the dust, and lifteth the needy out of the dunghill;" (8) "That he may set him with princes, even with the princes of his people.

Did you know that the scriptures reveal that the meek can be better understood as those broken in spirit before God? This includes people like Mary Magdalene or the woman at the well who has endured a terrible past. Beloved, these are the very people that God will use as instruments to reach others. In the next move of God, the "nobodies" will be placed before the "somebodies," and they will become "somebody" as they walk out of their shame and into their destiny. This will be the most significant move of God, which will usher millions into the Kingdom of God and will be known as the **"Revival of God's Glory."**

Beloved, it is essential to remember that God plans to use those often overlooked and undervalued to bring about significant change in the world. Just like in the story of the unclean lepers who were used to deliver a city, God has chosen to work through ordinary men and women of faith in a significant way. As the scriptures say, even the poorest among us can rise and become influential in God's kingdom.

The storms and trials of life are inevitable and designed to develop our character and test our faith. In these challenging times, we can draw inspiration from the life and sufferings of the Apostle Paul. He earned a place in God's Hall of Fame and provided us with the majority of the New Testament we have today. Did you know that the Apostle Paul suffered through several shipwrecks and was beaten until the bones in his feet were broken? But through it all, The Apostle Paul confidently proclaimed that the sufferings of this present world are not worthy of being compared with the glory that shall be revealed in us. (Romans 8:18)

Please remember that no matter how much trouble we may encounter, such as heartaches and sorrows, there is a reason and purpose for it. We can rest assured that our God is at work behind the scenes, honoring his word in Romans 8:28.

(Romans 8:28) "And we know that all things work together for good to them that love God, to them who are the called according to his purpose."

CHAPTER 6
YOU ARE SPECIAL

The scriptures teach that God, being Omniscient (All-Knowing), had foreknowledge of which individuals would choose to accept his plan to redeem fallen humanity and which ones would reject it. This means that even before the foundation of the world, God had already known the outcome of each individual's choice. While the offer of salvation is freely given to all, the sad reality is that most people would reject it. This is a sobering thought, as it highlights the gravity of our choices and the eternal consequences that come with them. Nonetheless, God's love and grace continue to be extended to all, and we must choose whether to accept or reject it.

We must understand that God's divine plan for us is in the Spirit. His Holy Spirit is in us enforcing this plan as Spiritual law, for he is the enforcer of Spiritual law. He will take charge, including control of the circumstances surrounding us, causing natural law to be for or against us. We were predestined to become his sons and daughters at the cross? God approaches us by preaching the cross, encouraging us to accept Jesus Christ as Savior and Lord. Accepting Jesus is the first step in God's plan, which was predestined for us before the foundation of the world.

Did you know that Wisdom in the word of God is referred to as God's Spirit? We need to learn from His great store of knowledge, and His counsel is always available to help us. This will make us much more robust than our enemy. Even though there is no book in the Bible with our name on it, the Holy Spirit can reveal our purpose and calling through His work within us. The Spirit of God was present with the Father when our life was planned. Did you know Jesus fulfilled enough scripture to be considered an impostor? Moreover, he fulfilled the law and its ordinances and sacrifices to put man's sins forward for another year and established a new covenant based on faith in him and his finished work. Through this covenant, man can have eternal life and be adopted into the family of God as required by a Holy God. The justice of a Holy God who is perfect in all his ways would not accept an innocent animal to redeem man's sins for eternal life, but God, in his mercy, gave his lamb as a ransom for all, and the sin debt was paid in full. The wrath of God was satisfied when his Son hung and died on that lonely Roman cross to pay the ransom debt for sin, making way for the fellowship that was lost through Adam to be restored through the sacrificial lamb of God. It is essential to understand that Jesus, also known as the other Adam, went through a trial, was found guilty, and was ultimately executed as a common criminal by being hung on a cruel Roman cross. Through this sacrifice, Jesus took upon Himself the sins of all humanity, past, present, and future, bridging the gap of fellowship back to God that was lost through Adam to be restored.

Did you know that God sacrificed His only Son so we may be adopted into His royal family as His children? Believers are welcomed into God's royal family through faith. This happens when we acknowledge our lost state and feel remorse for our sins. By accepting God's forgiveness for our sins and surrendering our lives to Christ, we allow Him to live through us. The main point of this chapter is that Jesus died in our place. As the scriptures state, "He who knew no sin was made sin for us so that we might become the righteousness of God in Him," bringing us into a new covenant with God through the Lordship of Jesus Christ.

When we accept Jesus into our hearts and lives, we are no longer our own but were purchased with a great price - the sinless blood of the Son of God. I want to emphasize the importance of having faith in God's love and how it can help us overcome depression and loneliness. God's love for us is immeasurable, and to demonstrate this love, He sent His only Son to die for us on the cross. This love allows us to become God's children and be adopted into His royal family, making us heirs to God's promises and blessings. Beloved, as joint heirs of Jesus Christ, we have been given the privilege of sharing in His inheritance. This means we have access to the same power and authority Jesus had during His time on earth. We have been given the Holy Spirit to guide, comfort, and empower us to live a life that honors God. Living a holy life guided by God's word is not always easy, but it is the most fulfilling and rewarding way to live.

Living a life that pleases God requires a daily commitment to seek God's will and obey His commands. It means putting aside our desires and aligning ourselves with God's purposes. But the good news is that we don't have to do it alone. God is with us every step of the way and promises never to leave or forsake us.

After finishing this chapter, I urge you to take some time to ponder on your personal life and ask yourself some critical questions. 1. Do you have complete trust in God's love for you? 2. Are you following His teachings to lead a righteous life?

If your answers were no to these questions, right now might be the right time to initiate a change. Consider it; God's love for you is so immense that He sacrificed His only Son for you. He desires you to experience life's true essence through a relationship with Him. Have faith in His love and commit to lead a life that honors Him. As children of God, we need to have a working relationship with Him. This relationship should encourage us to speak His word out loud into the atmosphere. We should declare that His promises and benefits are working within us while keeping in mind that God watches over His word to fulfill it. We should never forget that if God cares about the sparrows and knows when one dies, He cares about us, too. God is concerned about the well-being of those who have lost their life partner. He is also worried about those who have been incarcerated for their crimes against society, including the mothers who have sons facing death without a miracle of mercy from a higher court.

God is concerned about those who feel abandoned and alone. God is concerned about the well-being of those who have lost their life partner. He is also worried about those who have been incarcerated for their crimes against society, including the mothers who have sons facing death without a miracle of mercy from a higher court. However, God is concerned about those who feel abandoned and alone.

It's important to know that every person is essential to God, and He doesn't want us to live in bondage. Through the power and victory of the cross, our Savior dealt a mighty blow to humanity's sin. God raised him for our justification so we can enter His presence as someone without sin. Are you aware that those of us who have received salvation and acknowledge the free pardon of sin through Jesus Christ are declared righteous by his blood? Let me say that we must never give the devil an inch in our lives, for if we do, he will become our ruler, and the bible informs us that we are not ignorant of his devices which he uses to lure (*entice*) us to take the bait (*deception*) like an angler trying to catch a fish. We must remain vigilant as we navigate our adversaries' challenges and obstacles.

The enemy's traps may appear attractive and irresistible, but we must remember that falling into them will have serious consequences. Once trapped, we may find ourselves in a bondage that could take considerable effort and time to break free from. Therefore, we must exercise caution and make wise decisions to avoid becoming ensnared by the enemy's alluring but dangerous traps.

Beloved, we don't need external sources to predict our future. Instead, we should look within ourselves, find delight in our faith in the Lord, and seek introspection to know what lies ahead. As some people might think, our future is something other than what awaits us in the distance. Our future was placed within us at birth, and our loving Creator has given us the potential to become who we are meant to be and fulfill our purpose in life.

It's reassuring to know that our God will never abandon us and has promised to be with us till the end of time. We don't have to worry about our future if we have faith and trust in our Creator.

The main idea conveyed in this message is that our future is approaching us as quickly as we are approaching it. Additionally, did you know that God has a planned time for everything to happen? The scriptures state that God waited patiently for Noah to be born so that he could find favor in him. Noah's name means rest, which is significant in God's plan.

CHAPTER 7
WHAT IF MY PLAN FAILED?

Dear reader, how can I even begin to write about failures in life since, from a teen till a grown man, I have failed miserably in life? Still, you know what, dear reader? While on my way to minister to some drivers at our ACT Truckers Jubilee in Illinois, I had a visitation from the Lord, which helped open my eyes to how God looks at his children. Did you know that during that visitation, the Lord spoke in my spirit that he was pleased with me for where I am now with him, and He was pleased when I messed up during the past years of my life? I asked, "Lord, how could you have been pleased with me back then when I failed so miserably," he replied, "Because I saw your Heart!"

I have discovered through my Christian journey that for God to use us fully to be a successful witness to others, things may come the way that will cause us to question, like Job, "Why was I even born, and maybe it would be better if I was never born." (Is This You)

I have discovered that on some occasions, God will allow severe trials and obstacles to come against us, especially those of us chosen to accomplish great things in his kingdom, because he uses these trials to not only make us aware of the tactics of the enemy but to sharpen our senses to understand how important it is to stay on our assignment.

Through my years of experience, I have realized that God may allow various circumstances, people, and events to enter our lives for three reasons.

1. To educate us: Every situation and every person we encounter has the potential to teach us something valuable. Whether it's gaining knowledge, understanding a different perspective, or learning a new skill, these experiences contribute to our growth and development.

2. To teach us: Sometimes, we are presented with challenges and difficulties that serve as lessons designed to shape our character, deepen our resilience, and foster personal growth. These experiences, though often challenging, ultimately contribute to our maturity and wisdom.

3. To elevate us to the next level: In life, we encounter stepping stones that propel us towards our next level of growth, success, or achievement. These could be opportunities, relationships, or experiences that catalyze our advancement.

Reflecting on these reasons has helped me understand the purpose behind the various encounters in my life and how Grace has allowed me to approach them with a sense of openness and readiness to learn and grow. The truth is that God will sometimes allow things to come in a way that is fashioned to take us apart and break our will so that we can be put back together to operate in his will.

Beloved, we can illustrate this by imagining what it would be like to see a lovely home being refurbished. Think about someone driving by every day on their way to work and seeing work crews removing parts of the house could get the impression from all the debris scattered throughout the yard that the homeowner hired a wrecking crew instead of someone to restore and refurbish their home. Did you not know that everything must be inspected inside and out before restoring it? The bottom line is that the old must be checked and removed to ensure the foundation and joists holding the house together are in good shape. After completing all this, the home's desired appearance can be achieved, bringing the homeowner beauty, security, and comfort. (Is this your life?)

Dear reader, when God chooses an individual to fulfill a specific ministry position, He will allow that person to dismantle until nothing is left standing. This process is designed to refine and strengthen the individual's character, values, and beliefs in preparation for the challenges ahead. It is akin to military boot camp, where soldiers undergo rigorous training and conditioning to prepare them for the battlefield. This process aims to break down the soldier's will so that they do not react impulsively in battle but instead respond by their training. Likewise, the process that God allows individuals to go through when preparing them for ministry is intended to break down any pride, self-reliance, or other character flaws that may hinder their effectiveness in serving others.

Beloved, God's boot camp can be painful and challenging, but it is necessary to produce humble, compassionate, and mature individuals to fulfill their calling with excellence. It reminds me of the old saying, "If you want more power, turn up the heat to build the pressure.

God never promised a life free of troubles, but he promised that he would never leave us and that we would not have to face life's many trials alone. Therefore, to grow in our faith and be instruments in God's plan, we must be willing to withstand and overcome the complex challenges and tribulations we encounter. These trials can be likened to the intense heat of a furnace during times of affliction. We develop and strengthen our relationship with God through facing and enduring these trials with steadfastness, perseverance, and faith. We can find comfort in knowing that our compassionate heavenly Father has the wisdom to discern the perfect moment to pull us out of the trials and challenges we face, just like a skilled firefighter who knows the exact right time to rescue someone from a blazing fire. God sincerely desires to diligently train and prepare a cadre of seasoned warriors, using the trials of life to hone their skills and fortify their spirits to be ready for the imminent clash with the kingdom of darkness looming over us.

CHAPTER 8

THE WOMAN AT THE WELL

Did you know that John the Fourth chapter in the Word of God speaks of a Samaritan woman coming in the heat of the day who met Jesus in the desert called Jacob's well? Have you heard the story of how the scriptures speak about the Samaritan woman who had to come to the well in the heat of the day because she had a bad past of failed broken marriages; beloved, please know that God had a great plan for her life and her story made it in God's Holy book of fame that we call our bible?

Do you remember that she ran and told her story after meeting the Lord at the well? People who knew about her past failed marriages were touched by her testimony, which caused a whole city to come and see the Lord for themselves. This Samaritan woman, like some of us in this story, may have had a rough start in life. Still, in the end, she made it into God's book as one who could evangelize a whole city; therefore, may we use wisdom and listen to the person who made the statement, "Let us not despise the day of small beginnings!" The woman was looked down on as unfaithful. Still, God had a plan for her life because the scriptures declare that although the Jews had no dealings with the Samaritans, the needs of Jesus brought him through Samaria to set on that well.

Beloved, did you know that the Jewish rabbis of that day would usually tolerate up to three divorces? However, this woman had been married five times and was presently living with a man; therefore, her failed past made her stand out as an embarrassment or even a threat to others, and no doubt, she knew women would be gossiping behind her back. (Could This Be You)

This Samaritan woman may have had a slow start in life but made it into God's Hall of Fame. Like some of us, she no doubt grew up dreaming of someday becoming a happily married wife with a wonderful family. She may even have had a hope chest preparing for that particular day, which she would show her friends.

The Lord made the statements in John the fourth chapter that "his needs brought him to this woman in Samaria," which caused him to take the long route in his journey which caused him to journey through a hot desert to meet this woman who was going to be used of God to change the hearts and attitudes of an entire city. Please know that the people in Samaria were of mixed races of people, and the Jews were to have no dealings with them, but God had a plan for her life before she was born, and that same God has a plan for you. Dear reader, the Samaritan woman may have had grand plans for her life only to see them vanish. She has said "I Do" to five husbands only to watch her marriages fall apart with her dreams vanishing mid-air. (Is this You)

Notice, dear reader, because of her past, this Samaritan is no longer a respected woman in her community, and can you imagine how, before she met the Lord, she was dealing with low self-esteem and could not come to the well in the cool of the day like the other women because now she is living with a man that is not her husband? This woman was a broken vessel who had some knowledge of the coming Messiah and temple worship. However, Christ did not immediately bring up her past but asked the woman to receive Him and His gift without any prerequisite change that needed to occur in her life. <u>(God Can Make A Difference)</u>

Notice that after talking with the Lord about her situation, she was persuaded and believed that he was the promised messiah and her way of living would be changed forever. <u>(This can be You)</u>

Dear reader, I, like many others before me, can reflect on my life and find ways to identify with this woman, including her failures; however, I have decided that someone's opinion of me does not have to become my reality, and they certainly will not be the one that will sign my report card. I have been forgiven because my nature has been changed. Thank God I am no longer the trucker trapped in all my misery of uncertainties, but now I have meaning, hope, and purpose in my life while many others live in fear. <u>(I Know He Loves Me)</u>

CHAPTER 9

JUST BE YOURSELF

Growing up as a young teen, and like most teenagers, I experimented with drugs and booze, causing me to be in and out of trouble. Did you know that there came a time when my dad and mom were encouraged by our family physician and began making plans to send me to a psychiatrist? Still, I would have no part of it because I knew people who had been sent to these head shrinks, and these people seemed to be in their own little world.

As a young teenager, I never imagined seeking help from someone who listened to people's problems all day. I believed such a job would take a toll on the human mind, and I was afraid that reflecting on my early childhood would bring back too many painful memories. Furthermore, hearing about my friends' experiences with therapy made me feel uncomfortable, so I never considered this option. Beloved reader, I remember asking some of my friends concerning their recent sessions with a psychiatrist if they feel like they are getting the help they need, and I would usually receive different replies. Still, one reply got to me, for one of my friends stated that before they decided to see their psychiatrist, they did not want anyone looking at them or asking them simple questions.

Did you know that this emotional behavior is expected in our daily lives, especially with all the daily pressures of life? Therefore, did you know that the human personality is profound and beyond our imagination, and these professionally trained doctors are sometimes needed to help one confront things the patient is running away from but loves? The real problem is a problem of the heart.

Sometimes, what we think is helpful isn't helpful at all because it does not deal with the real issue, and that underlying real issue is sin; for beloved, because of the fall of Adam, sin entered the world and separated man from his fellowship with his creator. God says there is no good, and man's heart is deceitful and continually evil. (Jeremiah 17:9)

Moses gave the law to reveal to man that God is Holy and perfect, thus revealing that man born in sin cannot approach a holy, perfect God in his sinful condition.

The law was sent to diagnose man's sinful state and declare that sinful man must have a new heart to be accepted by a perfect, holy Creator. In ancient times, according to the law of Moses, families would offer an innocent lamb or dove as a sacrifice to seek forgiveness and atone for their sins, thereby avoiding God's judgment. This sacrifice served as a reprieve, delaying God's judgment against sin by symbolically transferring it for another year.

Did you know that God's most incredible creation, man, who was to be redeemed from Adam's fall, required God to sacrifice his only begotten Son to bridge the gap so that man could be declared righteous in his presence? God made an Everlasting covenant with his Son Jesus when he raised him from the dead and set him at his right hand in the heavenly places, far above all principality, power, might, and dominion, and every name that is named, not only in this world, but also in that which is to come: and hath put all things under his feet, and gave him to be the head over all things to the church, which is his body, the fulness of him that filleth all in all.

Did you not know that God made a way through the death, burial, and resurrection of his Son for man to receive a free pardon for his sin, and do not the scriptures declare that Christ who knew no sin was made sin for us and this beloved is called grace which we could never earn on our own merits? (2 Corinthians 5:21)

Did you know that Grace came through God's everlasting covenant with his Son, which satisfied his wrath toward sin? Because of this unmerited favor from heaven, man can now accept this free pardon and get a new heart to communicate with his creator. Once man receives this pardon and receives Christ into his heart, he can live a God-centered life. Jesus declared in (John 10:10) that he came to give life and that they can have that life more abundantly.

In other words, Jesus came and gave his life that we may have eternal life, which is a more and better life than we could ever imagine here and in the world to come, for beloved, Jesus gave this promise when he spoke of Himself as being the Good Shepherd of the sheep. Did you not know that it is only when we seek to follow God's direction for our life that we will bring glory to God? For beloved, I have found that the happiest people I know are those who no longer think of self and selfish desires because they have discovered that God is busy working in and behind the scenes to make their lives prosper. The law diagnosed our sin problem but could not give us a new heart, and aren't you glad that God's amazing grace was able to make way for us to receive a new heart and introduce us to the one who donated our new heart, and that is our savior, the Lord Jesus Christ. The Lord Jesus Christ not only gives us a new heart but he also comes to live in the life of the believer through his Spirit?

(Galatians 4:6) "And because ye are sons, God hath sent forth the Spirit of his Son into our new heart crying Abba Father."

Did you not know that this is why a vast, full-grown man will cry like a baby when they experience the presence of God's wonderful Spirit, for they realize that they are no longer their own but has made themselves available for the work of God that he may leave his signature through them to future generations?

People who have their mind centered on God tend to read their bible and pray daily, for their mind is upon seeing the kingdom of God flourish, for they are not concerned about satisfying themselves anymore but are determined to live a life of holiness and consecration to the Lord, realizing that this world is not their home and that because of their new heart, the world's view of life is different from theirs.

Did you know that a person who is centered on pleasing God will have a tender heart full of love and may sometimes even show emotion by crying, which is not a weakness but reveals the outward sign of a tender heart? Therefore, beloved, let us not be ruled or controlled by our senses but be thankful for a new tender heart that desires others to enjoy the freedom in Christ that we sometimes take for granted.

(Matthew 12:35) "A good man out of the good treasure of his heart bringeth good things, and an evil man out of the evil treasure of his heart bringeth forth evil things."

CHAPTER 10

WALKING IT OUT

I understand that embarking on anything new and unfamiliar is always challenging. Still, we must all embrace it for growth in the Christian life, which is abundant. Unlike the gifts of the world that expire and must be repaid with interest, God gave a gift that no earthly value can measure. He gave this gift from his heart with his heart thinking of the joy of having sons and daughters adopted into his royal family. The only obligation we have as the recipients of his gift is to decide to receive his gift of salvation so that we can dwell with him in eternal life, enjoying all the treasures and joys in the kingdom of heaven.

Did you know that during the early years of a child's life, they are both fascinated and afraid of the unknown? Similarly, Father God compassionately and lovingly cares for us with patience, knowing that as we come to Him, we are being transformed, and our sinful nature will daily pull at our mind with desires to turn away from God and return to a life of sin. I would like to encourage you to develop a daily habit of studying the word of God, and by immersing ourselves in the scriptures, we can saturate our thoughts in worship and praise, growing our understanding of God's goodness and grace.

By joining in fellowship with like-minded individuals, we can support each other in our spiritual journeys and find strength in our shared pursuit of truth and righteousness. As we deepen our relationship with God, we come to know Him more intimately, and we become increasingly aware of His love and grace. This knowledge strengthens us in comprehending our purpose and destiny better. It is like a baby born innocent and curious, exploring the world with wonder and amazement. Similarly, we can approach the marvels of God's creation with awe, eager to learn and grow in understanding His ways. Through the power of the Holy Spirit, we can be transformed from the inside out, becoming more like Christ with each passing day. This transformation happens as we surrender our will to God and allow Him to mold us into His likeness.

As we spend time praying and studying His Word, our hearts are filled with His truth, our minds are renewed, and as we grow in godliness, we become a light to the world. We show God's love and grace in all we do and share our hope in Christ. We live in troublesome times, and the scriptures instruct us to redeem the time for the days are evil. Let us commit ourselves to pursuing godliness, knowing that as we grow in His grace, we reflect His love to those around us.

Beloved, just like any relationship with someone we love, our relationship with God requires an investment of our time and effort. The more we invest in getting to know Him through His Word, the more we will become like Him, maturing into a righteous reflection of our Father's love. As we engage with the words of the Bible, we embark on a journey of discovering God's ways and His voice, which leads us to gain deep wisdom and an insightful understanding of His character and nature. Through this understanding, we begin to fathom His profound care for us and the entire world, guiding our daily lives and shaping our perspectives.

This knowledge transforms us from the inside out, changing our thoughts, attitudes, and behaviors to align with God's will. Through this transformation, we become beacons of light, shining the glorious light of the gospel for others who are lost and drowning in sin. As they witness the transformation in our lives, they will be inspired to pursue God's purpose for their own lives. In summary, our Christian growth depends on our commitment to spending time with God in His Word. As we get to know Him more intimately, we become more like Him, reflecting His love and light to the world around us.

CHAPTER 11

THE COMPASSION OF CHRIST

I want you to know that you are not reading this book by chance. I want you to know that God cares for his creation, and he cares about you. I can assure you that he is honest and has a plan for your life. You may not meet Angels in human form as I have, and you may not witness mighty miracles as I have, but let me assure you that God's love for you is beyond anything you could ever imagine.

Some individuals may experience confusion in their lives due to the absence of a tangible manifestation of God. Unlike a physician equipped with medicines and instruments who stands beside a patient in a hospital room, God does not physically materialize in this manner, making some people feel perplexed. God is a Spirit; we cannot see him with the human eye or travel to his heavenly office to present our case.

When I look back over my life and concentrate on some of the first notable miracles, I can sum it all up with compassion. God is a God that has compassion for his creation. I had just suffered through a seven-year nervous breakdown, and when God saw fit to reinstate me into his ministry, I was a renewed person who was full of compassion for God and his people.

I will never forget one incident at a hospital when God allowed me to feel his compassion. I was in the intensive care unit waiting room with friends. I kept noticing a young boy so hurt that I could feel his hurt. I asked around and discovered that his mother was in the ICU ward and was in a coma. One evening, I made it a point to speak with him. There was a church of God minister there who did not care for me because of what he had heard about me, but I swallowed my pride and reached out to the young boy. I informed him that I was a trucker evangelist, and God used me in the healing miracle ministry. I informed him that I felt his compassion for his mother, and if he agreed with me, I would pray the prayer of faith that God would, through his compassion, cause his mother to awaken out of her coma and be in her right mind. I informed him that I was leaving to fulfill an appointment to preach at my church but would return the next day to be with him.

When my feet entered the waiting room the next day, this young boy and several family members were jumping all over me, with some wanting hugs and others tapping me on the shoulder. The Church of God pastor was there with eyes big as small saucers, having played a significant role in the healing process. After a few minutes, the young boy said, "Preacher, I do not know who you are, but I know God hears your prayers. The young man went on to say that my feet had not left the hospital till his mother woke up out of her coma, and she woke up in her right mind."

The young boy said, “Preacher, you have no way of knowing this, but my mother had been in an accident in another state and has since been in a coma." He said, "The doctors had her moved to this state and this hospital, but she still showed no signs of recovery." He said, "Preacher, you prayed for her yesterday, and they had plans to take her off life support today.” The young boy said, "Preacher, after you prayed with me yesterday, she woke up, and she woke up in her right mind and knew me when I walked into her room." He said, "Preacher, we have been waiting for you, and my mother wants you to come to see her, and she wishes to thank you for reaching out to comfort me and pray such a beautiful prayer that so touched the heart of God that he moved to give me back my mother that I was not ready to lose.” When I stand in prayer lines praying for people, I expect God to meet them where they are. Pity and sympathy for hurting people are not enough. I feel the needs of the people before me, and I understand God's compassionate heart for his creation. My mentor, the late Apostle Don Stewart, taught me to realize that physical and spiritual healing are signs of our Savior's compassion for suffering humanity and spiritual resurrection by forgiving sins. This spiritual resurrection is about forgiving sins, restoring our relationship with God, and transforming our lives.

"Apostle Don Stewart emphasized that physical and spiritual healing demonstrates God's unwavering concern for the well-being of his creation and affirms his mastery over all the powers of evil that seek to undermine, defeat, and destroy us. I must tell you that our risen Lord has triumphed over all the works of the devil, and he reigns over our bodies just as he reigns over our entire existence." There have been times during a crusade when I have visualized the Lord Jesus watching me pray for the people. I could see him in spirit standing before me, touching the people and saying, "Be made whole." I don't know who you are, but I want to tell you that when we focus on Jesus instead of our troubles, worries, or sickness, we will see our creator, who carefully planned our lives before birth. Life is entirely of triumphs and trials. Like me, you may look back and see the scars of past mistakes and wonder, 'Lord, how could you use me in your ministry when my past seems to scream my unworthiness?' But let me assure you, God simultaneously sees the past, present, and future. Our mistakes do not limit his grace; it covers them all. He knew the depth of our failures and declared that his grace had declared us worthy. "God has chosen us, initiated the work of grace within us, and will bring it to completion. The love and forgiveness we receive from God are not determined by our past actions but rather by His constant, unwavering grace given to us without any conditions, and this grace can completely transform our lives, bringing us closer to him and drawing us to experience His divine presence in a greater way.

MY CONCLUSION

Dear reader, we learned throughout this book that salvation is a life-changing journey that involves understanding your new identity in Christ and making conscious choices to live according to your faith. After giving your heart and life to the Lord, you need to read the Bible regularly to gain insight into God's character and will for your life. This practice deepens your relationship with Him and guides daily living. Next, you need to search for fellow believers who can encourage you in your faith journey and look for opportunities to participate in small groups or Bible studies where you can learn from others and share experiences. Fellowship with other Christians strengthens your faith and helps you stay accountable.

The central message of this book emphasizes the challenges that new Christians may encounter after receiving salvation and how they can prepare themselves to confront and overcome the attacks of the enemy who seeks to lead them back to their old ways. It's essential to grasp that the journey doesn't culminate in salvation; instead, it marks the beginning. I advise you to seek opportunities for spiritual growth, such as participating in workshops, reading Christian literature, and engaging in discipleship programs offered by your church. Remember, the more you invest in your spiritual growth, the better equipped you will be to face life's challenges.

Dear reader, our identity and standing in Christ are paramount as they shape our beliefs, values, and purpose. These factors influence our actions, leading us to prioritize righteousness, love, and compassion. Ultimately, our choices and behaviors will refine, like metal tested by fire, to reveal their true nature and sincerity.

If this book has profoundly impacted your life or you recently decided to welcome Christ into your life, we would be overjoyed to hear from you. Your newfound journey with Christ is a significant step, and we would love to connect with you to offer support and celebrate this important milestone together. Your decision means a lot, and we are here for you every step of the way.

You can visit our USA Ministry website, where you will find a tab for free inspirational book downloads. Copy and paste this URL into your browser: www.witheredhand.org. Please go to the Contact Us page and fill in your contact information so we can celebrate with you. You can also email us at witheredhand.org@gmail.com. Please don't forget to check the website tab for our Monthly Newsletter, "The Hallelujah Times."

SCRIPTURAL REFERENCES

(2 Corinthians 5:17-18) (17) "Therefore if any man be in Christ, he is a new creature: old things are passed away; behold, all things have become new." (18) "And all things are of God, who hath reconciled us to himself by Jesus Christ, and hath given to us the ministry of reconciliation;"

(2 Corinthians 5:19-21) (19) "To wit, that God was in Christ, reconciling the world unto himself, not imputing their trespasses unto them; and hath committed unto us the word of reconciliation." (20) "Now then we are ambassadors for Christ, as though God did beseech you by us: we pray you in Christ's stead, be ye reconciled to God." (21) "For he hath made him be sin for us, who knew no sin; that we might be made the righteousness of God in him."

(John 3:16-17) [16] "For God so loved the world, that he gave him only begotten son, that whosoever believeth in him, should not perish, but have everlasting life"[17] " For God sent not his Son into the world to condemn the world, but that the world through him might be saved." This verse is a powerful reminder of God's love and the gift of eternal life through faith in Jesus. It encourages us to share this message of salvation with others.

(Romans 8:1-2) (1) "There is therefore now no condemnation to them which are in Christ Jesus, who walk not after the flesh, but after the spirit." (2) "For the law of the Spirit of life in Christ Jesus hath made me free from the law of sin and death."

(Romans 8:3-7) (3) "For what the law could not do, in that it was weak through the flesh, God sending his own Son in the likeness of sinful flesh, and for sin, condemned sin in the flesh:" (4) "That the righteousness of the law might be fulfilled in us, who walk not after the flesh, but after the Spirit." (5) "For they that are after the flesh do mind the things of the flesh; but they that are after the Spirit the things of the Spirit." (6) "For to be carnally minded is death; but to be spiritually minded is life and peace." (7) "Because the carnal mind is enmity against God: for it is not subject to the law of God, neither indeed can be."

(Romans 8:8-12) (8) "So then they that are in the flesh cannot please God." (9) "But ye are not in the flesh, but in the Spirit, if so be that the Spirit of God dwell in you. Now if any man has not the Spirit of Christ, he is none of his." (10) "And if Christ be in you, the body is dead because of sin; but the Spirit is life because of righteousness." (11) "But if the Spirit of him that raised Jesus from the dead dwell in you, he that raised Christ from the dead shall also quicken your mortal bodies by his Spirit that dwelleth in you." (12) "Therefore, brethren, we are debtors, not to the flesh, to live after the flesh."

ABOUT THE AUTHOR

This author suffered through more than seven years of mental illness, which caused him to leave home and travel the continental United States and Canada in an 18-wheeler, attempting to drive his life away to discover his true identity. He was but too frightened to know who he was, for there was a little boy inside him who had been abused all of his life, causing him to be angry at the world.

During this time, the author begins to encounter Angels of God who look human, but he discovers they knew way more about him than he knows about himself. In one encounter, the man disappeared mid-air while walking away with nowhere to go.

These encounters, which could be compared to the TV show "Touched by an Angel," helped prepare the author to minister for more than twenty years throughout the streets of the inner cities of America. This journey often brought him face-to-face with danger and violent gangs. Yet, with unwavering courage, the author, wearing his famous Indiana Jones hat, usually fed and clothed people experiencing homelessness, including going under bridges and abandoned houses, including a few crack houses. His ministry was a testament to the love of Jesus, reaching out to hurting people who would sell their souls for a dollar.

In 2024, Dr. Jerry W. Hulse proudly holds the esteemed position of an International Evangelist representing Miracle Life Church International Ministry. This ministry, which originated in the Philippines under the leadership of the late A.A. Allen and continued by the late Apostle Don Stewart, has seen significant growth after Dr. Jerry and his beautiful wife Augustina committed to the Lord's call on their life. Since March 10, 2022, Dr. Jerry and his wife, Augustina, have been based in the Philippines, where they have been actively involved in monthly revivals nationwide. Overcoming significant personal challenges, Dr. Jerry is now recognized as a Life Coach, a Mental Health Coach Advocate, and a Board-Certified Mental Health Coach with Life University and the Association of Christian Counselors. His contributions have been widely appreciated, as evidenced by the honorary doctorate in philosophy and theology from Kingdom Ambassadors University.

For those who want to gain personal insights into Dr. Jerry's work and life, he shares his experiences and teachings on his YouTube channel, "Jerry & TinTin Hulse." Dr. Jerry has made significant contributions to spiritual literature, having written and contributed eighty-eight sermons to SermonCentral.com. Those interested in exploring his messages can search for his name, "Jerry Hulse," using the website's search bar.

SPECIAL RECOGNITIONS

Evangelist Jerry's books are trendy and highly sought after by viewers tuning in to the TV program "Pickin' Time with Bob" on Living Faith TV in Abingdon, Virginia. Bob and Laurie Smallwood confirmed the tremendous demand for Jerry's books. In 1995, Bob encountered Jerry on a snowy night in the mountains of Virginia. Driving his 18-wheeler back home from the northern states, Jerry provided vital assistance by guiding Bob through a heavy snowstorm to Interstate 81. This allowed Bob to check on his Rural Retreat, Virginia radio station. Subsequently, Jerry's visit led to a live radio interview on Bob's station, eliciting an enthusiastic response from the audience. This fateful meeting ultimately sparked revivals that left a lasting impact and continue to be remembered and discussed today. **Bob & Laurie Smallwood.**

"We met Evangelist Jerry Hulse in the middle of 2017 at a Don Stewart workshop in Phoenix, Arizona." There was such an anointing on Jerry that caused us to want to know more about him, and we are glad we did. That divine encounter has developed into a beautiful friendship. We count it a blessing to be asked to read and comment on this anointed book. We are proud to say that Evangelist Jerry is an anointed man of God with the pen of a ready writer as he takes us into the importance and power of maintaining a close relationship with the Lord through a devoted life of consecrated prayer- **CALVIN & VERONICA MOORE** ***(Word of Fire Tabernacle Church, Los Angeles, California)***

Tin and I would like to give special recognition to **Chaplain Mark Hewitt** & The Road Angel Truckers Center at exit sixty-eight (68) off Interstate seventy (70) in Brownstown, Illinois, USA. Thank you, Chaplain Mark, for being such a great friend and distributing our books to the visiting drivers. The Road Angel is a trucker's oasis along Interstate seventy that provides free counseling home-cooked meals, showers, and overnight parking for the motoring public. Give them a call: **+1 618 427 3737**

Dr. Jerry W. Hulse, ordained as an International Evangelist, proudly represents Miracle Life Church International Ministry, a ministry founded in the Philippines by the late AA Allen and Don Stewart. Bishop Filipe Ping and Nida Alba now oversee Miracle Life Church International. Since March 10, 2022, Dr. Jerry and his wife TinTin have traveled, conducting monthly revivals and crusades throughout the Philippines.

Augustina and I are thrilled to acknowledge W.V. Grant and his beautiful, anointed wife, Milly Grant. Brother Grant is the Founder and President of W.V. Grant Ministries and the senior Pastor of Eagle's Nest Cathedral, an incredible spirit-filled church at 1440 Regal Row in Dallas, Texas. In January 2022, Brother Grant accurately prophesied the exact day God would send me to the Philippines, including when they would remove the visa requirements for entering the country.

Augustina and I give special recognition to our dear friend, minister, and recording artist, **Brother Caleb Howard**, and his wonderful family. We were blessed to minister with him in Siargao Island, Philippines, and we are still receiving good reports from that meeting. For more on him, subscribe to his newsletter at **www.calebhowardminitries.com.**

My wife Augustina and I offer special thanks to Withered Hand Ministries, Inc. in Bristol, Tennessee, for their prayers and support. Dr. Jerry founded this 501c3 ministry in 2004. WHM is overseen by WHM President & Treasurer **Robert E. Hale**, who resides in Bristol, Virginia. We want to include his awesome helpmate, our dear friend **Becky Hale.**

We express our gratitude to the Pastor of our home church, Pastor Bishop Bryan Henson, and his wonderful family. Bishop Bryan Pastors at Miracle Life Church in Fortune Valenzuela Metro Manila, Philippines. Pastor Bryan is Miracle Life NCR District's district director and Pastors at the Miracle Life Church in Fortune Valenzuela Metro Manila, Philippines. **bryanrhenson@gmail.com**

We sincerely thank **Dr. Ronylo Adorable** and his incredible family. Bishop Adorable is the General Secretary of Miracle Life Church International and the Pastor of one of the Miracle Life Churches in General Santos, Philippines.

We wish to recognize a dear friend, **Evangelist James Green,** from Seattle, Washington. Brother James is a man of faith and the founder of Earthshakers International Ministry. We have ministered together several times in the Philippines and highly recommend him to your church. Brother James hosts a live call-in conference line on the call-in church every Friday at 7 p.m. Eastern Time. The call-in number is **563-999-1229. No pin is needed.** **https://www.earthshakersint.com**

We want to acknowledge **Apostle Wesley Hobbs** for his inspiration and guidance. Brother Wesley has consistently accurately conveyed messages from the Lord to us. Brother Hobbs is the Founder, Director, and CEO of God's International Ministries in Tulsa, Oklahoma. You can receive a blessing by viewing and subscribing to his YouTube channel.

We want to acknowledge **Pastor Randy Brokaw** from Saginaw, Michigan. Pastor Randy is affiliated with the Church of God and oversees Free Indeed International Ministries, a thriving ministry that reaches people worldwide. His ministry is known for its numerous healings, signs, and wonders, including creative miracles.

We thank our dear friends, **the Osborne family**, at the Gospel Bookstore at 2130 Euclid Avenue in Bristol, Tennessee, USA. We thank them for carrying our books in their bookstore. I used to purchase hundreds of prayer clothes from this store with scripture verses printed on them. Look them up on Facebook and tell them Jerry and Tin say, "Hi." **+1 276-466-5249.**

We give a big shout-out to **Mrs. Ellen Reed & her Husband**, the owners of Storyteller & Jackrabbit Java Books located on Broad Street in Thermopolis, Wyoming, USA, for carrying our books. **+1 307-864-3272**

We give a shout-out to **Heaven's Gate Christian Bookstore.** The bookstore is at 151 Industrial Blvd. in Eatonton, Georgia, USA. Tin and I wish to give them a big shout-out for carrying our books in their bookstore. **+1 706-923-1992**

I wish to honor my incredible wife, **Augustina M. Hulse**, for her unwavering love and support. I am truly blessed to have a wife devoted to the Lord who exudes passion for conducting revival services. Her invaluable contributions in designing book covers and overseeing publications have been instrumental. My beautiful wife, fondly referred to as TinTin, epitomizes the virtues of a Proverbs 31 woman.